W9-AZE-786

THE
WIZARDS'
HANDBOOK

DR. ROBERT CURRAN

First edition for North America published in 2011 by
Barron's Educational Series, Inc.

Copyright © 2011 Marshall Editions

All rights reserved. No part of this book may be
reproduced or distributed in any form or by any means
without the written permission of the copyright owner.

All inquiries should be addressed to:
Barron's Educational Series, Inc.
250 Wireless Boulevard
Hauppauge, NY 11788
www.barronseduc.com

ISBN-13: 978-0-7641-6408-8
ISBN-10: 0-7641-6408-2
Library of Congress Control Number:
2010933311

M MAGB

Conceived, designed, and produced by
Marshall Editions
The Old Brewery
6 Blundell Street
London N7 9BH
www.marshalleditions.com

Commissioning Editor: Laura Price
Design: Duncan Brown – The Book Makers
Picture Manager: Veneta Bullen
Production: Nikki Ingram

Date of manufacture: November 2010
Manufactured by: 1010 Printing International Ltd.
Color separation by: Modern Age Repro House Ltd.,
   Hong Kong

Printed in China

10 9 8 7 6 5 4 3 2 1

THE
WIZARDS'
HANDBOOK
Dr. Robert Curran

BARRON'S

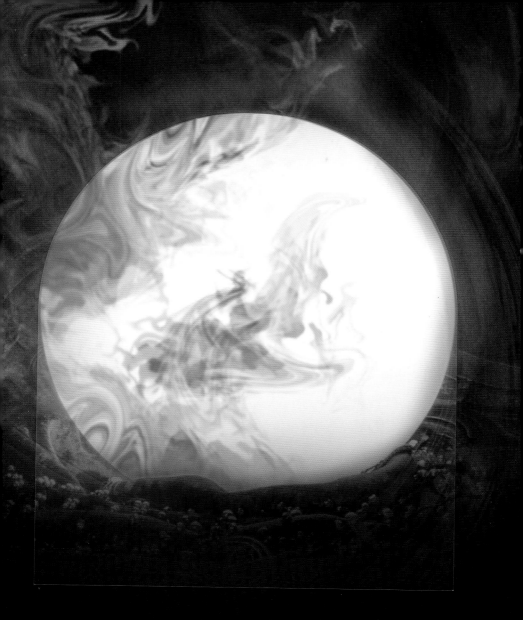

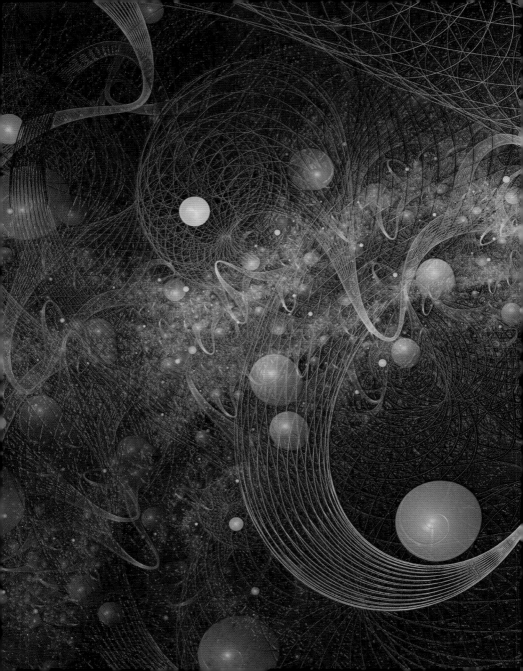

THE EARLY WIZARDS

Where does magic come from?
And who were the earliest magicians we
know about? And, most importantly, why did
humankind develop such a fascination for
the occult and the forces of nature
beyond their control?

EARLY MAGICIANS

Early humans lived lives of fear and uncertainty. With danger at every turn from the powers of nature and wild beasts, these men and women turned to greater powers in an attempt to ease the hardships of their lives.

From the earliest times of humankind, men and women came together in groups and tribes. For most, they faced a very hostile landscape. There were storms, floods, droughts, forest fires, and wild animals to threaten their lives, and the constant possibility of death made them very aware of their own weakness and frailty. These early

ABOVE *Amazonian hunting parties faced dangers of all sorts – from leopards to crocodiles and from floods to fire.*

peoples were heavily dependent on what they could catch by hunting; if they failed, they would starve. They also believed that spirits and forces lived in the landscape around them – in rocks, trees, rivers, mountains, and the sky. These spirits were not always helpful to humans, but some humans found they might be pleaded with, tricked, or bribed into kindness.

LEFT *Early tribes recorded hunting successes and their experiences in the natural world in cave paintings. It is possible that these drawings had a more mystical purpose than simple decoration.*

It eventually occurred to our early ancestors to ask, "What if we could use the forces that lie in the natural world to make life better for ourselves?" And so the first concept of magic was born.

Among many tribes there developed those who were able to contact and communicate with the spirits and control the world around them for good. They began to take on an important role – becoming

RIGHT *A messenger between the human and spirit worlds, a shaman was said to treat illness by mending the soul.*

what are known today as *shamans* or *witch-doctors*. They were, to some extent, the "middle men" between the human and the spirit world and could change things to benefit their neighbors.

There was, however, another more fearsome side to this magic. If the shamans could use their skills for the benefit of the tribe, they might also be able to use it for darker purposes, especially against those who angered them. Such men (and some women, too) were able to wield great power within their tribal groups as fear of their powers grew.

The earliest magic practiced was probably the casting of spells to control the weather and aid successful hunting. Spirits were called on to calm strong winds that ruined crops and make sure that plenty of game was found on hunting expeditions.

Later, these magicians began to predict the future – when the best time was to hunt, what the future held for the chieftains and leaders – and these predictions, if proved true, made the wizards even more important to the tribe.

They also became healers, studying the local herbs and plants and using them to cure injuries or illness or calling on the spirits to heal the sick.

RIGHT The darker side of the shaman was often in evidence, as in this very threatening leather mask.

Despite this, many practitioners of magic were simply regarded as "wise" men and women who had special knowledge. The word "wizard" wasn't used to describe them until much later – possibly several thousand years after these early tribes existed in the early medieval period. There are many arguments as to where the name came from – some say it came from the Middle English word *wys*, meaning "knowledgeable," while others have suggested that it might even be Lithuanian, coming from the word *zinoti*, meaning "to know" (particularly to know the future or to know secret things). In this case, the earliest wizards were simply fortune-tellers and healers, and the word "wizard" was not used in connection with magic or wonder workers until the early 1500s.

As might be expected, it did not take long for the magicians' craft to become shrouded in ritual, such as speaking certain words and performing certain actions, usually in secret. It was this secrecy that led to the idea of magic as a mysterious skill, and the magicians became a breed apart – so much so that ordinary folk revered and feared them.

Nowadays, the word is applied to a variety of magicians and conjurers, including illusionists on television and even Harry Potter ("the boy wizard") – a very long way from those early herbalists and weather forecasters, indeed.

THE DRUIDS

In the ancient Celtic world of Western Europe, a group of people, mostly men, held great supernatural power over their tribes. These were the Druids, the holy people of the ancient Celts.

There has been much argument over the exact origin of their name – some scholars say that it comes from a very old language that existed long before the Celtic peoples and was originally *drui-wid-s* (an oak-knower – referring to their sacred tree); others say that it comes from the ancient Welsh *dryw* (meaning foreteller or seer – one who sees the future); but many say that it comes from the Old Irish *drui* (meaning sorcerer).

However they got their name, the Druids were supposed to be the protectors of very dark and mysterious secrets, and as such they wielded great

power amongst the kings and leaders of Gaul (France) and the British Isles. They interpreted the will of the Celtic gods and spirits with whom they were familiar, and no king or local ruler could afford to anger them, for while they were healers who saw the future and could encourage crops

to grow and cause enemy's crops to die, they could also devastate a land with plague and bring famine and destruction at will.

The descriptions we have of the Druids come mainly from the writings of the great Roman general, Julius Caesar. He fought against the Celts in Gaul between 58 and 51 B.C. and encountered Druids in battle. He describes them as stately and dignified men in white robes, possibly with long beards, who cut mistletoe (a plant sacred to them) with a golden sickle at certain times of the year to harvest its magical properties. This portrait may not be entirely true, as the Druids had to climb the trees to cut the mistletoe, and to do so in robes would have been nearly impossible.

The Druids, as much as the Celtic generals, controlled the army and were said to be able to aid them by magically creating mists in battle to confuse their enemies.

The writings from the Roman armies who later invaded Britain under Claudius Caesar in A.D. 43 depict the Druids in less flattering ways, describing them as tribal medicine men with painted faces and half-naked bodies that were hung about with grisly ornaments.

Lᴇғт *Magical mistletoe was sacred to the Druids for its mystical properties.*
Rɪɢʜт *According to the accounts from the Roman legionnaires in Britain and Gaul, the Druids were bearded sorcerors in flowing robes.*

When the Romans attacked the stronghold in Anglesey in northern Wales, the Druids screamed hideously, covered themselves in ashes from sacred fires, and made magical signs in the air, but to no avail. The Romans destroyed many sacred Druid sites and turned others over to the worship of their own gods.

In Ireland there are also accounts of female druids, known as *drui-ban*. Just as powerful as the male magicians, these wizardly women usually focused their powers on prophesy (Caesar mentions three Gaulish women called *dryads* who were great seers), and some of the later sorceresses are believed to have become Irish Christian saints – for example, St. Bridget, who established a nunnery at Kildare.

But all was not good magic for the Druids. Some scholars have suggested that they

practiced (or oversaw) human sacrifices. For instance, at Magh Slecht, the Plain of Adoration in Ireland (now Tullyhaw, County Cavan), there was once said to be a great circle of stones and, in the center of the circle, small children were sacrificed to the Crom Cruach (the Bowed God of the Mounts).

When Roman rule took over in northern Europe and the word of Christianity spread, the time of the Druids finally came to an end. Some Druids still exist today but their modern role is purely ceremonial. In Wales, for example, they are now largely regarded as custodians of the Welsh culture, but who knows how many still hold the mysterious knowledge of their ancient counterparts.

LEFT AND RIGHT *Druid human sacrifice took different forms. Victims were burned alive inside a "wicker man" (left) or killed with a sacrificial knife (right).*

KAHINS, FUGARA, AND MUQARRIBUN

Strange things live in the deserts of the Middle East. They make their presence known by little swirls of dust and sand, moving across the bleak and empty landscape at terrific speeds.

Some say that they are merely tiny dust storms created by the eddying winds, but others seem to think that they are the *djinn*, the demons and spirits of the desert. Creatures of ferocious magical powers, the *djinn* are believed to be fallen angels or beings that have never been born; as such, they are incredibly hostile to humans. Local people tend to stay away from them or make protective mystical signs as the dust clouds pass.

There are, however, those who say they are able to communicate with the *djinn* and possibly, at times, control them. These *djinn* masters are usually the descendants of the Bedouin, a tribe of people who live in the Middle Eastern deserts and whose origins go back into the sands of time. Before the Islamic faith spread across many Middle Eastern countries, certain mystical practitioners could be found in the market squares of the great cities. These *kahins*, or "oracle-mongers," claimed to have a special relationship with the *djinn*, who told them the secrets of the future.

Strange and mystical, the *kahins* wandered into the deserts from time to time to speak with the *djinn*, and they returned to tell fortunes and make prophesies. Some were even able to perform inexplicable magic feats. It was a dangerous path to follow, however, for the *djinn* could turn on them at any time and there

RIGHT *In the fairy tale, Aladdin forges a special relationship with a djinn that he discovers in a lamp.*

ABOVE *The Bedouin tribes wandered the Sahara desert, where their shamans were said to hear the voices of the* djinn.

are tales of *kahins* being ripped to pieces by the invisible talons of the desert demons.

Out in the desert, among the Bedouin, other types of magicians were living. These were the *fugara* or medicine men – there were some women as well – who were able to heal any sickness and find lost objects. Many were said to have received special powers from the *djinn* they encountered in the desert, but others were the descendants of ancient Bedouin tribal shamans. They relied on herbs and potions made from rare plants found in the bleak deserts, which the *djinn* revealed to

them, and they were said to hear the voices of the spirits on the desert wind whispering strange secrets to them. All *fugara* were considered great sorcerers of the time.

Perhaps the most sinister and fearsome of all the Middle Eastern wizards were the *Muqarribun*, the eerie ghost priests of southern Jordan. These dark, veiled men were usually of Bedouin origins and could talk not only to the *djinn*, but also to the ghosts and spirits of the dead. Consequently, they had great knowledge of magical forces. They tended to live in isolation not far from Wadi Rum, a great rocky outcrop in south Jordan in the Middle East. Legend says that this is all that remains of the demon-city of Irem, a great structure built by the *djinn* in the days of King Solomon, which was destroyed by Allah. However, the magic of the *djinn* survives there, and it is from this that the *Muqarribun* draw their formidable powers. It is believed that there are ancient books hidden in the area that contain an ancient, evil knowledge that the ghost priests can consult at will, striking fear into the hearts of all who meet these dark magicians. Who can know what strange powers exist under the endless desert skies?

ABOVE *It would have taken great courage to consult some of the* djinn, *particularly if they were as evil-looking as this demon!*
BELOW *In the Middle East, priests, like this one in Jerusalem, took many forms and included the dark magicians, the Muqarribun.*

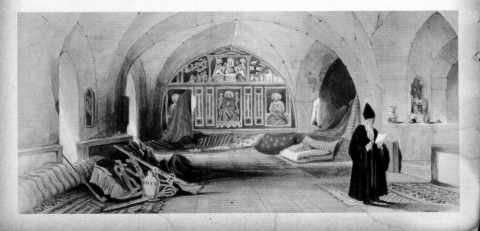

THE ALCHEMISTS

Today, we tend to think of alchemy, the forerunner of modern chemistry, as medieval foolishness, with long-bearded men crouching over boiling pots and jars, endlessly trying and failing to turn lead into gold. However, alchemy is far more steeped in mystic history than that.

The word "alchemy" comes from the ancient Arabic *al-kimia*, which is both a way of thinking and a process largely connected to turning ordinary metals into gold and finding something that will make men live longer. It has been practiced for almost as long as there have been civilizations – in ancient Mesopotamia, ancient Egypt, Persia (modern Iran), Korea, China, Japan, and ancient Greece and Rome. Indeed, alchemists may have been stirring their potions and reciting their incantations for at least 2,500 years.

Their belief was that all things in heaven and earth were somehow connected, and that one element of the world, be it stone, rock, or wood, might be magically or chemically changed into another, such as gold.

During the medieval period, large "schools" of alchemists, many using ancient documents kept safe through the ages, were founded all over Europe. Most had one goal in common – the transmutation (change) of a base metal, such as iron, into gold (the process of *chrysopoeia*) or silver (the process of *spagyric*).

The other role of the alchemist was to search for an elixir (a potion) that would make them live much longer than normal – possibly forever – *and* keep them young; this was known as the Elixir of Life. Much of their work was carried out in secret,

RIGHT *During the Middle Ages, alchemists devoted their lives to the search for the secret of how to change base metals to gold.*

for the Church disapproved of such things – life and death were God's domain. In fact, Pope John XXII issued a Papal Bull (a decree from the Church) forbidding anyone from attempting the "alchemical arts." This meant mortal danger to anyone caught doing so!

Two great goals of medieval alchemy were to discover and use the Philosopher's Stone – a substance which could transmute any substance into precious metal – and the Emerald Tablet which, if eaten, would grant eternal life to whoever discovered and took it. Several alchemists claimed to have found these incredible objects, but there was no evidence to support their claims.

The search for these mystical wonders led to many more common, and perhaps more successful, experiments that have found their way into chemistry today. These include the creation of gunpowder; the sterilization processes; the creation of dyes, paints, and cosmetics; and many more side-products that are still in use in the modern world.

One of the great alchemists was the English philosopher and Franciscan monk Roger Bacon

LEFT *In their search for the Philosopher's Stone, medieval alchemists experimented by heating up all kinds of explosive and potent mixtures.*

(1214–1294), who is generally credited with the "creation" of gunpowder in Europe. Although a monk, and therefore banned from such practices, Bacon was widely believed to have found the Emerald Tablet. Indeed, according to some sources, he may still even be alive today. However, evidence suggests that he probably died in 1294, and when he did, he left behind a body of work that inspired all alchemists who followed him.

Another famous alchemist of the 1500s was the mightily named Philippus Aureolus Theophrastus Bombastus von Hohenheim (1493–1541) who was, thankfully, better known as Paracelsus. Besides alchemy, he was also interested in the occult and is supposed to have left behind several books of alchemical spells that the Church declared as being almost books of witchcraft. However, he did suggest several new ideas about medicine and pioneered the use of chemicals in healing.

Throughout history, many charges were directed at the alchemists, who became tinged with magic of the foulest kind (or so the Church alleged). One of these charges was that they usurped God's status not only by transmuting metals but

ABOVE *An alchemist's workshop was full of jars that contained strange specimens – to add to that hanging from the ceiling!*

also by creating life in their alembics (special sealed jars). Indeed, many drawings of ancient alchemists *do* show strange beasts suspended in jars of fluid. Religious authorities became convinced that alchemy was the Devil's work and sought to ban it. However, the alchemists banded together in secret societies and communicated by publishing obscure books full of mystical imagery that concealed their true purpose in secret code and symbol. It is just as well that they did, for the works of the ancient alchemists laid the foundations for modern chemistry.

SECRET MAGICAL SOCIETIES

Magicians and wizards did not always work alone. Across the centuries there have been stories of groups who practiced magical arts – and they may exist today!

THE TEMPLARS

The Templars were a medieval order of monkish knights within the Christian church who were suspected of worshipping dark gods and practicing magic to gain money and influence. Formed around the time of the First Crusade in 1119, their original mission was to guard pilgrims on their way to the holy shrines. They were given the Temple Mount in Jerusalem as their headquarters, reputedly the ruins of the old Temple of Solomon. Here, they are said to have found various magical items and books that they brought back to Europe, which made them extremely powerful.

Accused of witchcraft in 1305 by Philip IV of France, many of them – including the senior figures of Jacques de Molay and Geoffrey de Charney – were burned as witches.

THE ASSASSINS

From around the late eleventh century, a mysterious cult of killers existed in the Middle East. These were the Assassins, the followers of Hassan-i-Sabbah, a strange and intriguing figure from whom they take their name, according to some historians. They were skilled in all forms of killing, usually by stealth and in secrecy, and were also supposedly skilled in potions and poisons, which gave them a reputation for sorcery.

It was believed that they took certain herbs that gave them visions of Paradise and other worlds. Some people suggest that they had the power of invisibility, which added to their mysterious skills.

THE ILLUMINATI

By the late 1700s, peoples' minds were already starting to dismiss magic and look toward science for explanations of the world. However, one group of men sought to fuse magic with science for their own political ends. They were formed in May 1776 in Ingolstadt, Bavaria and called themselves "The Ancient and Illuminated Seers of Bavaria" (or "The Illuminati"). Their purpose was to control the world by magical and scientific means.

They called on an ancient knowledge that enabled them to place themselves in very high commercial, religious, and political positions all across the world. Indeed, there are some who claim that they are still in power now.

FAR LEFT *Templar magic was considered evil by those who feared their growing power.*
LEFT *A knights templar coin depicting the quest for the holy grail.*
ABOVE *The pyramid and the all-seeing eye, symbols used by the Illuminati sect of Bavaria.*

THE NECROMANCERS

Necromancy is an ancient form of magic that involves summoning the spirits, or sometimes the actual bodies, of the dead and manipulating them to the wizard's will. Necromancers are always regarded with fear and, in 1456, the Christian writer, Johannes Hartlieb, defined necromancy as demonology, or the study of demons.

Some of the earliest references we have to the summoning of spirits come from ancient Babylonia, where sorcerers, called *manzazuu*, brought ghosts and spirits (the *etemmu*) back from the grave, usually for the purposes of predicting the future. It was believed at that time that the dead could foresee what was to come. The rituals for raising *etemmu* sometimes included wearing the dead person's clothes and eating black and unleavened bread. Romans and Semitic peoples usually called on great prophets and heroes to reveal what the future held. In the Bible, the Witch of Endor brings back the spirit of Samuel, and in the ancient Greek tales of the Odyssey (written around 700 B.C.), the wanderer Odysseus brings back the spirit of the prophet Tiresias to discover what will become of him and his crew.

During the Middle Ages, the art of necromancy was strongly connected to witchcraft and was punishable by death. Indeed, the word changed to nigromancy, meaning "black," and strange and foul rituals were connected with it. This did not prevent people from continuing to practice it. Dr. John Dee, who was connected to the Royal Court of Queen Elizabeth I, and his assistant, Edward Kelley, were supposed to have raised a spirit in a London churchyard (see pages 50–53).

Today, necromancy is a central part of the religion of Quimbanda, which is practiced in Brazil, and it is associated with animal sacrifice and witchcraft. So it seems that the dark arts of the ancient necromancers may still be practiced today.

LEFT *Necromancers practice hydromancy (divination by means of water) and pyromancy (divination by means of fire).* BELOW *The Witch of Endor conjures the spirit of Samuel.*

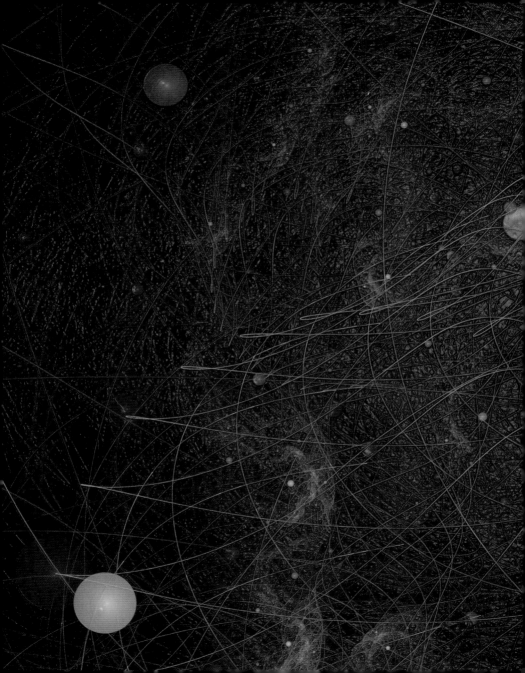

THE
GREAT
WIZARDS

History is filled with tales of mighty wizards and acts of unbelievable magic. From controlling the natural world to raising the dead, from seeing the future to shapeshifting sorcery, here are some of the most famous and infamous wizards the world has ever known.

CAThBAD The DRUiD

Of all the Irish Druids, perhaps the most famous is Cathbad. Allegedly a powerful figure in the Royal Court of the Kingdom of Ulster at Emain Macha, he is sometimes described as "the Irish Merlin," although perhaps he is not so benign. His name appears in the great Myth Cycles that describe the earliest times in Ireland.

Cathbad was said to be the Chief Druid or advisor to Conchobar mac Nessa, the great king of Ulster, although he is difficult to pin down, as the tales about him show him in different guises. Some say that he was actually Conchobar's father and that, in an earlier time as a *fian* (a landless warrior), he had taken the king's mother, Ness, during a raid.

Whatever his background, Cathbad was said to have great powers, such as being able to turn grass and twigs into fully armed soldiers and having the power of prophesy. In one tale, a baby girl was born to one of the great Irish families. The child, Deirdre, was predicted by Cathbad to become the most beautiful girl in Ireland. But she would also bring great sorrow and harm to the country.

King Conchobar had Deirdre hidden away on an island and raised only by an old woman. When Deirdre grew up, the king sent a spy to see if she was as beautiful as Cathbad had said. The spy was overcome with her beauty and returned to tell the king that she was very plain, hoping that the king would allow her to return from isolation. However, Cathbad revealed her true beauty to the king and Conchobar, in turn, fell in love

Right *Naoise carries Deirdre away in their fruitless attempt to escape the wrath of Conchobar.*

with her. Sadly, Deirdre already had another love, Naoise, one of the Sons of Usna, so she rejected the king and fled with her beloved and his two brothers, who helped the lovers escape.

On realizing the king had been deceived, Cathbad conjured a lake of slime that trapped them all.

In his fury, Conchobar had Naoise executed and, in her grief, Deirdre killed herself.

The story of Deirdre and the Sons of Usna is one of the Great Sorrows of Irish storytelling, and Cathbad's magical role in the downfall and death of the lovers is a low point in Druidic lore.

MERLIN

Of all the magicians in history, perhaps none is more famous than Merlin, the wizard of the legendary King Arthur.

Although best known as Arthur's magician at the Court of Camelot, Merlin also had strong connections with two other British kings – Gwenddolau and Vortigern. It is possible that the mighty Merlin acted as an advisor to three great British kings.

Nobody knows who Merlin's actual father was, or if he shared parentage with the rest of his family. Some say that he was a *cambion* – a half-human/half-spirit creature. According to some stories, Merlin and two of his brothers were either soldiers or commanders at the Battle of Arderydd (or Arfderydd) in Scotland. There, Gwenddolau's forces – known as "the six loyal companies of Britain" – fought those of Rhydderch Hael, King of Dumbarton. The monarch and both of Merlin's brothers were killed, leaving Merlin grieving for them all. Such was his sorrow, it is said he went mad and fled to live in the forest like a wild man – tended only by his sister, Gwenddydd – and became known as "Merlin Wyllt" or "Wold," meaning "wild."

While living in the forest, it is believed that Merlin befriended the ancient gods and forces that dwelt there and from whom he acquired great knowledge – more so than any other living man. This made him the greatest magician of his age and,

when he came to his senses once more, he became known as "Merlin Emrys" or Merlin the Wise.

So great was his fame and wisdom that he came to the attention of a British king, Uther Pendragon – King Arthur's father. Uther sought out Merlin as a counselor and advisor and brought him to his court. The link between Uther and Merlin comes from an old text known as *The Auchinleck Manuscript*, which was written in the thirteenth century but probably comes from a set of older texts detailing stories about Uther and his court.

At court, Merlin is said to have

RIGHT *Merlin the Wise was advisor to both King Uther and his son Arthur.*

ABOVE *Merlin (center) tutored Authur (left) from a young age.*
LEFT *Merlin used his magic to help King Uther to seduce King Gorlois of Cornwall's wife.*

performed many great and mystical deeds for the king, whose forces seem to have been continually at war with those of King Gorlois of Cornwall. One such deed involved creating a magical fog to confuse the Cornish soldiers; another was to deceive Gorlois' wife into thinking that King Uther was actually her husband so she would bear him a child. This child would eventually become King Arthur.

Merlin – now known as "Merlin Ambrosius" – was widely regarded as one of the greatest wizards in Britain. When Uther died and Arthur succeeded him, Merlin became the king's advisor once more. With Merlin's help and counsel, Arthur united many of the squabbling kingdoms under him and began to forge a proper, stable monarchy.

All the while, Merlin's magical powers continued to grow. He was said to be able to make himself invisible, change shape, and summon storms, often gaining Arthur military victories through his formidable skills. There seemed to be little that he couldn't do. However, as he grew older, Merlin

appears to have grown increasingly foolish. Despite his great powers and his position at Arthur's court, it seems that the wizard was lonely and like many other men, craved the love of a woman.

As Arthur's kingdom became more settled and was not often at war, there was little for Merlin to do except continue with his magical studies. Then he fell in love.

The object of his affection was a younger woman named Vivien, who was herself a sorceress with some power, which she often used for evil. It is said that she attempted to ensnare Merlin with her own magic in order to obtain his occult knowledge. According to legend, she was secretly in love with Arthur and was jealous of Merlin's influence on the king. Thus, she set out to learn a particular spell from Merlin that she could turn against him and therefore trap him forever.

Vivien began to tell wicked tales about King Arthur's knights, but Merlin was able to answer all of her accusations, except one. When she said that Sir Lancelot was secretly in love with Arthur's wife, Guinevere, and she with him, Merlin could not deny the truth of it, so he gave himself to the sorceress and told her the spell to keep the secret love from the King.

Triumphantly, she turned him into an oak tree to stand entrapped forever. In other versions of the story, he turned himself into a tree out of grief and shame at having betrayed his Queen.

It's possible, of course, that Merlin didn't really exist, at least not in the way we think about him. It's quite probable that he wasn't a single man at all but was rather created from stories about a combination of men who were extremely wise or who were believed to be great magicians. The number of names and nicknames by which Merlin is known would certainly suggest this. Gradually, these stories have all been drawn together and their heroes have become a single figure – the one passed down to us. But that doesn't diminish the mystery and the magic. No matter how we think of him or if he really existed in the way that we believe, Merlin still remains the greatest wizard of them all.

Left *In old age, Merlin fell helplessly in love with a young sorceress called Vivien.*

HERMES TRISMEGISTUS

Of all the great wizards in history, none is more mysterious than Hermes Trismegistus. It is not known for sure if he even existed, and if he did, was he a human or was he actually a god?

His name (which translates as the "thrice-great Hermes") gives us no clue, as it seems to suggest the Greek god Hermes, who was the messenger from the supernatural world. We do know that Hermes Trismegistus may have been worshipped in the ancient world, perhaps even as a god himself. He might even have been a combination of *two* gods – the Greek Hermes and the Egyptian Thoth, the gods of writing and magic, respectively – and this combined deity was worshipped in the Egyptian city of Khemun, which the Greeks called Hermopolis.

This being combined many of the ancient wisdoms and knowledge, which were passed on to his followers. Archaeologists have also found reference to a deity who was worshipped in southern Greece called Ti-ri-se-ro-e, or Trisheros, who may also have been this mighty being. He is portrayed in some writings as a great hero, a great scholar, and a great ruler, giving him the nickname "Three Times Great" (*Trismegistus*). There is evidence that many of the Greeks, and later the Romans, were not terribly keen on the worship of such a god or demi-god and actively tried to suppress it.

There are others, however, who say that Hermes Tristmegistus was an actual person and that he might have come from the Middle East. Tradition and legend says that he may have lived at the same time as the patriarch Moses and may have actually known him. From the patriarch, Hermes learned much of the secret knowledge, which Yahweh (God) had passed down to Moses, and he wrote it down in a series of

ABOVE *Hermes Trismegistus was worshipped in the temple of Hermopolis in Khemun, Egypt.*

scrolls and texts. Others still say that he was a great Islamic philosopher who was able to discern things that were beyond the knowledge of ordinary men. But nobody knows who he was for sure, although he is also believed to have written a vast number of texts.

Many of these texts were said to have turned up in medieval times to become the reference works for wizards of the time. The entire body of work is referred to as *The Corpus Hermeticum*, but this is just a catch-all phrase for the body of work. The books were said to have contained great and magical secrets, such as the secret of turning metals into gold (much sought after by the alchemists) and of living forever.

95

ⲁ̄ⲛⲉⲥⲙⲟⲩⲓⲛ̄ⲁⲩⲁⲩⲣⲁⲕⲩⲝⲥⲟ ∴
ⲡ̄ⲣⲟⲧⲟⲩⲙⲉⲁⲡⲉⲗⲟⲅⲏⲥ
ⲟⲩⲕⲉ̄ⲧⲓⲟⲩⲙⲏⲩⲟⲩⲁⲣⲉⲝⲥⲟ ∴
ⲩ̄ ⳿ⳁⲟ̅ ⲧ ⲉ ⲧ ⲛ . ⲗⲁⲗⲏ ⲗⳁⳁ
ⲡⲟⲩⲉⲥⲩⲛⲩⲟⲩⲥⲉⲙⲩⲛⲁⲥⲟ
ⲙⲉ ⲓ̈ ⲛⲁⲓ ⲕⲁⲓ ⲡⲣⲟⲟⲥⲭⲣ̄ⲥⲁⲙⲉⲛ
ⲕⲁ ⲉ ⲓ ⲟ ⲛ ⲕ ⲟ ⲩ ⲟ ⲥ ⲓ ⲛ ⲉ ⲥ ⲉ ⲕ ⲗ ⲟ ⲥ ⲉ
ⲱ̄ⲙ ⲟ ⲩ
ⲕⲁ ⲓ ⲁ ⲩ ⲏ ⲅ ⲁ ⲣ ⲥ ⲩ ⲃ ⲉ ⲕ ⲗ ⲁ ⲕ
ⲕ ⲟ ⲩ ⲧ ⲁ ⲭ ⲁ ⲓ ⲛ ⲁ ⲱ ⲫⲉ ⲓ ⲁ ⲱ
ⲉ ⲁ ⲓ ⲁ ⲛ ⲁ ⲱ ⲧ ⲟ ⲛ ⲭ ⲟ ⲩ ⳁ ⲗ ⲩ ⲟ ⲥ ∴
ⲕⲁ ⲓ ⲁ ⲛ ⲟ ⲃ ⲩ ⲟ ⲃ ⲛ ⲓ ⲙ ⲉ ⲁ ⲩ
ⲧ ⲟ ⲓ ⲟ ⲛ ⲭ ⲁ ⲱ ⲙ ⲟ ⲩ
ⲕⲁ ⲓ ⲕ ⲁ ⲛ ⲁ ⲟ ⲑ ⲱ ⲥ ⲁ ⲩ ⲓ ⲁ ⲩ
ⲙ ⲁ ⲧ ⲁ ⲓ ⲟ ⲙ ⲟ ⲩ
ⲕ ⲁ ⲓ ⲃ ⲩ ⲉ ⲩ ⲁ ⲣ ⲃ ⲩ ⲉ ⲓ ⲥ ⲧ ⲟ ⲟ̅
ⲙ ⲉ ⲙ ⲟ ⲩ ⲁ ⲱ ⲙ ⲁ ⲕ ⲁ ⲓ ⲛ ⲟ ⲩ
ⲙ ⲉ ⲙ ⲟ ⲩ ⲟ ⲛ ⲧ ⲟ ⲟ̅ ⲉ̄ ⲙ ⲟ ⲩ ∴
ⲟ̄ ⲩ ⲟ ⲣ ⲧ ⲁ ⲓ ⲡ ⲟ ⲝ ⲗ ⲟ ⲓ ⲱ ⲁ ⲓ ⳁ ⲟ
ⲃ ⲛ ⲑ ⲏ ⲥ ⲟ ⲩ ⲧ ⲁ ⲓ ⲱ ⲉ ⲁ ⲓ ⳁ ⲧ ⲓ
ⲟ ⲩ ⲟ ⲓ ⳁ ⲃ ⲁ ⲛ ∴
ⲙ̄ ⲁ ⲕ ⲁ ⲣ ⲓ ⲟ ⲥ ⲁ ⲙ ⲏ ⲣ ⲟ ⲟ̅ ⲗ ⲓ
ⲧ ⲟ ⲟ ⲛ ⲟ ⲙ ⲁ ⲕ ⲩ ⲉ ⳁ ⲧ ⲁ ⲓ ∴
ⲕ ⲁ ⲓ ⲟ ⲩ ⲕ ⲉ ⲧ ⲉ ⲩ ⲗ ⲉ ⲩ ⲯ ⲉ ⲱ ⲟ

رأمهلين لكماأكون
متيح قتل ان اذهب
ولا اكون ايضا
مزمور داود النبى ٣٩

انتظارا انتظرت الرب فنظر
إلى واستجاب دعوتى
صعدنى من جبّ الشقا
ومن طين الحياه
اوقف على الصخره
رجلاه وسهل خطاىى
وسبّ فى فمى حمدا
جديدا وتسبيح لالهنا
ينون كتيرين
فيخشون ويتوكلون
على الرب طوبا
للرجل الذى اسمه الرب
رجاه ينظر فى

This latter secret was supposedly contained within a text called *The Emerald Tablet of Hermes Trismegistus* or *The Secret of Hermes*. A good number of the texts were supposed to deal with alchemy, and indeed the name of the mysterious figure has passed into modern chemistry when we speak about containers being "hermetically sealed."

There are even more mysterious books that are attributed to Hermes Trismegistus. However, some scholars have argued that these are no more than fragments of an Arab book, the *Kitab sirr al-asrar* (the Book of the Secrets of Secrets), which was written for the guidance of rulers in the Middle East. Nevertheless, parts of this work were translated into Latin as a "secret magical book" by the monk John of Seville around 1140. It is quite possible that many of the writings that are credited to Hermes Trismegistus were, in fact, written by other people around perhaps the third and second centuries B.C. They certainly seem to suggest a number of styles and origins.

ABOVE *The combination of the gods of magic Thoth and Hermes, Hermes Trismegistus was a powerful figure.*

LEFT *Very few parchments like this fragment of the Psalms of the Prophet David in Greek and Arabic have survived to modern times.*

His work, however, has remained popular through the ages, and even today there are a few modern societies that bear his name and pledge to delve into "secret and ancient knowledge." Whether or not they can is another issue.

So who was Hermes Trismegistus? Was he a god or simply a man who possessed knowledge beyond the range of most mortals? Whoever he was, he still remains a mystery.

NOSTRADAMUS

One of the greatest powers of any wizard, it is said, is the ability to predict the future. Indeed, many magicians gained both their status and fame in this respect. And one of the most famous of these must be the French apothecary (chemist) Michel de Nostredame, often known by the Latin rendering of Nostradamus.

His book *Les Propheties* is still in print in various languages, as are various books about it, offering a number of interpretations concerning its contents.

Michael de Nostredame, the son of a grain dealer and public notary (an official who witnessed signatures on legal documents), was born in 1503 in the town of St. Remy-de-Provence in the South of France. His father, Jaume de Nostredame, was believed to have been Jewish and may have been interested in Hebrew mysticism before converting to the Catholic faith. This may have given Michel a background in secret teachings in obscure language forms as he grew up.

At the age of fifteen Michel entered the University at Avignon, where he studied grammar and logic. However, he was forced to leave the academic life when the University had to close

Le Medecin guarissant phantasie Purgeant aussy p drogues la folie.

in 1521 because of a fearful plague that was raging in the surrounding countryside.

He began to study medicine on his own, going around the locality collecting cures and remedies and then using them himself and passing them on to other people. He did this for eight years until he applied in 1529 to study medicine in the University of Montpellier. His career there was short-lived when he was expelled from the University

LEFT *This portrait of Nostradamus was painted by his son, Cesar Nostradamus.*
ABOVE *In sixteenth-century France, apothecaries usually provided the medical care for the community.*

because he had been an apothecary (and some said an alchemist), which was a "base trade" and not allowed under the University's rules. However, after his expulsion, he continued to heal and produce his own medicines and may even have called himself "Doctor" (which he was not allowed to do). He was also said to have invented a curious pill that protected people against the worst effects of the plague, which was still raging in some parts of France.

Between 1531 and 1547 he traveled around southern France, making potions against the plague in places such as Marseilles and Aix-en-Provence. Finally, in 1547 he settled down in the town of Salle-de-France, where he married a rich widow (he had been married before but had lost his family to the plague) named Anne Ponsard. At the same time, his interests were drifting away from formal medicine toward the occult and magic. It was around this time that he changed his name from the French de Nostredame to the more important, Latin Nostradamus. Going with the trend at the time and with his new wife's money, he began in 1550 to publish a series of almanacs that contained prophesies for the future.

The first almanac, written in very obscure language (the style of which he may have learned as a child in his Hebrew learnings), was set out in quatrains, just like poetry, and was a great success. Encouraged, Nostradamus began to publish more. In total, he published 6,338 prophesies, which stretched

PORTRAIT
DE MICHEL NOSTRADAMUS,
Astronome célèbre.

Michel Nostradamus naquit à Saint-Remy, petite ville de Provence, le 14 décembre 1505, à l'heure de midi ; il était fils de Jacques Nostradamus, notaire royal de cette ville, et de damoiselle Renée de Saint-Remy ; il était petit-fils, côté paternel que maternel, de médecins et mathématiciens célèbres ; il fut reçu docteur en l'université de Montpellier, dont il exerça la charge de professeur. Ce grand homme a vécu sous les règnes de Louis XII, François Ier, Henri II et Charles IX, dont il fut médecin ; il retourna à Salon, nouve ville de Provence, et y mourut en bon chrétien, après avoir été tourmenté par la goutte qui, dégénérée en hydropisie, le suffoqua au bout de huit jours, ayant prédit l'heure et le jour de sa mort, qui arriva entre trois et quatre heures du matin, le 2 juillet 1566.

LEFT *In France, Nostradamus was feted as a man of many talents – here as an astronomer.*

ABOVE *Nostradamus' reputation was enhanced by his invention of a "pill" to protect against the plague.*

far beyond his own time and into the distant future. Because they were written so obscurely, the exact meaning of these prophesies has been the subject of debate even up until today.

Nostradamus died of gout and associated illnesses in 1566 and left behind a reasonable fortune to look after his wife and step-family. Those who study his work say that they can trace the influence of some earlier, end-of-the world prophets and that much of it should not be taken seriously at all. They claim that Nostradamus was just a showman who was rather full of himself. Others, however, are not so sure. Maybe Nostradamus actually could see the future and maybe he knew more about it than we suspect; as such, he still remains a mystery.

Dr. Johannes Faustus (Faust)

Perhaps one of the best-known magicians is the sinister figure of Dr. Johannes Faustus, or Faust, as he is sometimes known. Stories, books, plays, and even an opera have been written about him and have made his name famous all across the world. And yet we are not even sure if he existed.

was able to summon the Devil through magic arts and who struck a deal with the forces of Hell, enabling him to enjoy earthly pleasures at the expense of his soul. The story inspired many writers and poets to retell his tale, and the name has become linked to deals with the blackest of magic. But did Dr. Johannes Faustus exist?

The story of Faust is probably not German at all but may be based on an old Polish folktale. This story concerns a Polish wizard named Pan Twardowski who was greatly skilled in Black Magic. We do know that he may have actually existed, as there are references to him living in Krakow around the end of the fifteenth century and is described as a German immigrant of high rank.

Using a fearsome, iron-bound book, Twardowski is supposed

The name "Faust" gives us no clue – it is simply the German word for "fist," although it can also mean "lucky." Faust's story, however, concerns a sorcerer who

Left Faust is often depicted as a learned man.
Above This illustration of Faust in Hell is from the score for Berlioz's opera The Damnation of Faust.

ABOVE *In the German legend, Faust uses his powerful magic to summon the Devil.*

to have summoned the Devil and demanded a life filled with wealth and power in return for his soul. He promised the Devil that he would surrender his spirit to the Infernal Realm, but only in Rome (a place that he had no intention of visiting), and this was written into their agreement.

Aided by the Devil, Twardowski enjoyed a life of great luxury and became exceptionally famous – so famous, in fact, that he became a senior courtier at the Court of Sigismund II Augustus, King of Poland, and was able to gain further favor by influencing the monarch after the untimely death of his wife, Barbara Radziwill.

In order to console the King, Twardowski went to buy him some wine and stepped into an inn named Rzym, near the center of Krakow. Immediately, the Devil appeared and demanded his soul – Rzym in Polish means "Rome," something the magician hadn't considered.

Despite his protests, the Evil One bore him away, but as he did, Twardowski cried out to the Virgin Mary, begging her for help. She did so and the Devil was forced to drop the wizard onto the Moon, where he still lives today. His face can be seen looking wistfully back toward his homeland every night.

The tale of Twardowski may have been adapted by German storytellers, and the name of Dr. Johann Faustus, who may well have been a German magician, was substituted. It first appeared as a chapbook (a pocket-sized book that was popular at the time), written by an anonymous author and detailing the life of a certain Johann Georg Faustus. It was roughly a retelling of the story of Twardowski, which was said to have occurred around the same time.

The German version certainly attracted a great deal of interest and provided inspiration for works by a number of artists, musicians, and writers. The most famous of these was the Englishman, Christopher Marlowe (1564–1593), whose play *The Tragical History of Doctor Faustus* was published in 1604, eleven years after Marlowe's own mysterious death. Many thought that the play might have been about Marlowe himself, as he was also thought to have been a magician. However, despite all of this interest, the figure of Johannes Faustus remains as enigmatic as ever.

BELOW *The popular Faust legend has been depicted by many different artists through the centuries.*

DR. JOHN DEE

Perhaps one of the most mysterious and magical figures at the Court of Queen Elizabeth I was Dr. John Dee, who was often referred to as "the Queen's Wizard."

The son of a minor courtier, Dee was born around 1527 and grew up to become one of the most learned men of his time. He was very skilled in mathematics (which many common people at the time thought was very close to Black Magic), and in 1554 he was offered a scholarship at Oxford University in England, which he turned down.

In previous years he had become interested in magic and the occult, and between 1540 and 1550 he had traveled across Europe speaking to wizards and so-called "men of lore," allegedly gaining many of their secrets, becoming interested in astronomy, and predicting the future

-ABOVE *John Dee was held in high status as a scholar who was versed in both science and magic.*

from the movements of the stars. Studying mathematics, it seems, was no match for the appeal of wizardry for Dee.

In 1555, he was arrested and thrown into prison by the then Queen, Mary I, for casting a horoscope that predicted the monarch's death and her half-sister Elizabeth taking the throne (which *did* happen). Mary later pardoned him and he returned to his mysterious studies. Dee now claimed that he was able to contact ghosts and angels by means of certain spells and that they would reveal to him secrets of the future and maybe even influence present events. When Mary died in 1558, her half-sister did take the throne and Dee was appointed to the Royal Court, where he was even allowed to calculate the date for Elizabeth's coronation. Some people say that he was a magician there. Others say that he was a secret agent in the style of James Bond and that he continued to travel to Europe and meet with

BELOW *At court, Queen Elizabeth often relied on John Dee's advice on political and diplomatic matters.*

ABOVE *A depiction of John Dee and Edward Kelley raising a spirit from the grave in London.*

government's policies, particularly with regard to Spain, with whom England did not have good relations. Whether this is true or not isn't clear, but it is thought that the Queen took great note of what he said.

In 1582, John Dee met and became friendly with a certain Edward Kelley (also known as Edward Talbot), who considered himself to be a magician, although his motives were highly questionable (he may have been more of a trickster). Along with Kelley, Dee conducted a number of experiments around London, including visiting several graveyards around the city to try to raise the spirits of the dead to make them reveal future events. As he grew older, Dee was becoming more and more obsessed with talking to ghosts and angels, but he was also concerned with the alchemists' dream of turning base metals into gold.

Kelley claimed to have found a magic book – *The Book of Dunstan* – in the ruins at Glastonbury, which Dee began to translate in order to reveal "wonderful secrets." In 1583, he and Kelley and their families traveled to the Continent with Prince Albert Laski, a Polish nobleman, in order to find a wealthy nobleman

strange and mysterious people. And he maintained his interest in magic and the supernatural.

At all times, Dee carried with him a peculiar stone that he claimed was his "scrying crystal" (scrying was a way of predicting the future by looking in a mirror, precious stone, or reflective surface) and that if he looked into it and said the right incantations, angels would reveal what was to come. It is said that he was often consulted by the Queen's ministers to help determine the to finance their activities. There, they met Emperor Rudolph II in Prague, and King Stephen Bathory in Poland, but neither man was impressed by John Dee.

He returned home, disillusioned to find that his great library of magical works, which he had built up over his life, had been ransacked and many of the books stolen. This was to continue from time to time (it may well have been that Kelley was behind it).

Nearly destitute and with Kelley now gone, Dee appealed to Queen Elizabeth, who made him Warden of

Christ's College, Manchester, but he didn't like this work. When James I came to the throne in 1603, he was unsympathetic to Dee, and the wizard moved to Mortlake, where he died in 1608 or 1609.

RIGHT AND BELOW *In later life, John Dee claimed that angels such as Cassiel, Gabriel, and Raphael dictated several books to him.*

Sunday	Monday	Tuesday	Wednesday	Thursday	Friday	Saturday
Michaël	Gabriel	Camael	Raphaël	Sachiel	Anaël	Caffiel
name of the 4 Heaven	name of the 1 Heaven	name of the 5 Heaven	name of the 2 Heaven	name of the 6 Heaven	name of the 3 Heaven	No Angels ruling above the 6 Heaven
Machen.	Shamain.	Machon.	Raquie.	Zebul.	Sagun.	

POPE FORMOSUS

Although today we think of the Pope as being a holy person, this has not always been the case. In fact, over the centuries a few Popes were thought to be dark magicians who had risen to the Papacy through the application of magic, using this power for their own ends.

Popes such as Anacletus II, whose name was struck from the records, Honorius III, and Sergius II were supposed to have written grimoires (books of Black Magic), which were used by witches.

The most evil of all was said to have been Formosus, who reigned as Pope between A.D. 891 and 896. He seems to have been a very colorful and political character who had been excommunicated (cast out of the Church) by Pope John VIII for plotting against him in 872 while still only a bishop. Formosus was later reinstated in the Church in 883 by Pope Marinus I, but it was what happened to him after his death that is truly bizarre.

In 897, under the orders of one of his successors, Pope Stephen VI, the body of Formosus was dug up, dressed in full ceremonial robes, and was put on trial before a full college of cardinals. The now rotting corpse was accused in court of political wrongdoing, heresy, and witchcraft. It was alleged that Formosus was a mighty sorcerer and that he had performed some very powerful spells. One of these was rumored to be the magical construction of a speculum vitae, or magic mirror, in which he could see everything happening in the world and use this knowledge to gain great personal power. But the mirror had another, darker purpose. It is said that Formosus, through his great magical skills, drew down a demon from the Otherworld – the stronghold of the spirit world – and trapped it in a prison beyond the glass, using its power for his own evil ends.

The trial of the dead Pope was known as the Synod Horrenda, or Cadaver Synod, and must have been

LEFT: *It was claimed that Formosus had harnessed the power of a demon for his own ends.*
ABOVE: *Formosus dressed in the Pope's formal regalia.*

a terrible sight. Pope Stephen (who is generally supposed to have been crazy) accused the corpse of all sorts of evil things and appointed a Cardinal to answer on its behalf. Naturally, the corpse was found guilty. It was stripped of its robes, had the first two fingers of its right hand (with which the Pope gave a blessing) broken, and it was thrown into the Tiber River in Rome. The corpse was later "saved" by a hermit and reburied. A few years later, Formosus was pardoned by Pope Theodore II; the body was dug up yet again and reburied in St. Peter's, the resting place of Popes.

Those who put the corpse on trial did not prosper. Within a year, Stephen was thrown into prison, where he was strangled. Following his death, the Papacy fell into turmoil for many years.

But what of the mirror with its imprisoned demon? It is said that Formosus's immediate successor, Boniface VI (an elderly and timid man who reigned for only 16 days in April 896), had the mirror removed from Rome to stop its evil influence from polluting the city. He commanded the mirror be taken to "the ends of the Earth" (perhaps Britain or Ireland – the location is really not clear), where presumably it still lies. Although the next Pope, Stephen VI, did try to retrieve and destroy the mirror, it has never been found.

ABOVE *The corpse of Formosus must have been a grisly sight as the trial, the Cadaver Synod, got underway.*

So was Formosus really an evil magician, or was it just a story created by his political enemies, including Pope Stephen? And is there really an enchanted mirror lying somewhere in the world with a terrible demon still trapped inside? And could that demon ever be released? Hopefully we'll never know for sure.

THE EARL
OF DESMOND

Even though history will tell you otherwise, it is well known all across Ireland that the Great Earl of Desmond still lives in his sunken castle deep beneath the waters of Lough Gur in County Limerick.

Of course it is difficult to tell exactly which Earl of Desmond it is, since all the stories about him are conflicting and contradictory. The Earls of Desmond were the Fitzgerald family who held lands in Munster and considered themselves one of the last great families of the old Irish Gaelic nobility. They were also a turbulent family with several members only holding the title very briefly before losing it to another, meaner member of the family. Some have suggested that the "Great Earl" was Thomas Fitzgerald (1453–1534), but most agree that it was probably his cousin Gerald Fitzgerald (1533–1583), who was a notable warrior and, some say, a magician.

It is quite probable that the Earl was an alchemist, but from the many

tales told about him, he was also a wizard who performed great feats of supernatural magic. It was claimed that he could make himself invisible, fly through the air like a bird, and change shape at will. He concocted strange potions and salves that changed the perception of reality, and he owned a magic mirror that showed him events occurring all across the world.

The Earl lived in a sinister castle on a tiny island in the middle of Lough Gur and

Left *Alchemists studied natural phenomena.*
Right *Snakes and lizards were part of the toolkit.*

in the tallest of its dark towers he had a magic workshop in which he drew and conversed with demons from the Outer Reaches of time and space. There was no end to the Earl's powers.

When the Earl of Desmond married, his new wife was a lively and inquisitive woman. She had heard all the rumors about her husband and was anxious to see his diabolic workshop for herself. Each evening when the Earl retired to his room, his wife begged and pleaded to be taken with him. He always refused, but she was extremely persistent and, at last, he relented and agreed to her wish.

However, there were rules. He told her that she must not make a sound no matter what she saw – if she did, it would be bad for her and for him – and must not move from where he placed her. Agreeing to it all, the Earl's wife followed him to the sinister chamber, where strange things stirred in jars of viscous fluid and alembics seethed and sizzled.

Placing his wife in the center of a protective circle and instructing her not to set foot outside it, the Earl stood in the middle of the room and suddenly changed shape several times, becoming a great serpent that filled the room, a leprous hag who hobbled around the edges of the circle, and a great vulture that spread its wings over her. Terrified, his wife bit her lip until the blood ran but uttered not a sound.

Slowly, the Earl returned to his human form but his head and feet immediately began to expand. This proved too much for his wife. She uttered a dreadful scream and, with a clap of thunder, the castle and everything in it sank beneath the waters of Lough Gur. And there, people will tell you, it remains to this day.

Locals swear that the Earl still conducts his sorcerous experiments in the depths of the lough, riding out from time to time into the wider world to snatch away the strongest man, the most beautiful girl, or the greatest scholar in the area to imprison them forever in his underwater fort.

Even today, you are advised not to wander the shore of the lough in case the wizardly Earl snatches you into a watery tomb.

RIGHT *Wizards as powerful as the Earl of Desmond were said to be able to conjure up all kinds of things, including this hand from within a circle of fire.*

ISAAC LURIA

Although many of the most famous European wizards tend to come from Christian backgrounds, the Jewish faith also had its sorcerers. Usually these tended to be great Rabbis (Jewish teachers) with supernatural powers who used their "secret knowledge" to influence the wider world.

One of the most famous of these Rabbis, and one who is said to have had the most influence on Western magic, was Isaac Luria (or Yitzhak ben Shlomo Ashkenazi, to give him his Jewish name), a teacher from Safad in the Galilee area of Palestine – which was under the rule of the Ottoman Turkish Empire at the time.

Luria lived from 1534 to 1572 and was considered to be a great Jewish mystic and scholar of the occult. He studied the Kabbalah – a mystical book said to be full of secret knowledge passed from God to the founders of the Jewish faith, Abraham and Moses – and also the *Zohar* (the *Book of Splendor*), which contained some powerfully secret instructions about the creation of life.

Luria is also said to have dealt with *dybukks* (Jewish demons) from the very edges of reality, but being a very holy man they could not harm him.

It is said that his teachings, which used material taken directly from the secret books, influenced many other Jewish magicians around the same time, especially in Europe. One of those rumored to be influenced by Lurianic thinking was Rabbi Judah Loew ben Bezalel, the sixteenth-century Maharal (leading religious teacher) of Prague. He is believed to have secretly constructed a Golem – a great figure of clay – which he brought to life by a secret

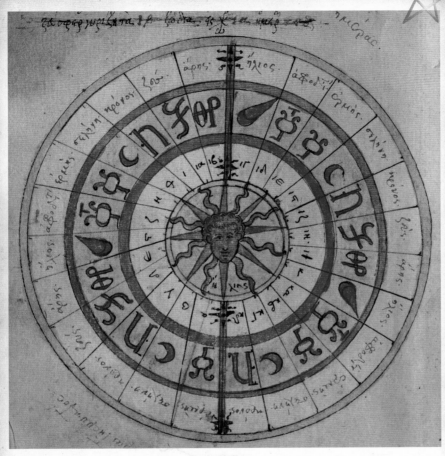

ABOVE *The secret symbols of the Kabbalah were said to contain great knowledge passed directly from God.*

word and then allowed to run amok. Rabbi Luria is supposed to have left behind some scrolls containing all sorts of magic secrets. These are believed to have passed into the hands of Luria's foremost disciple, Hayyim ben Joseph Vital, but were said to have been destroyed after his death. Maybe they are still somewhere out there waiting to be discovered, along with all their dark secrets.

Nicolas Flamel

*Alchemist, truth-seeker, devout Roman Catholic –
Nicolas Flamel became famous for discovering the power
of the Philosopher's Stone.*

Anyone who has either read the book or seen the film *Harry Potter and the Sorcerer's Stone* will be familiar with the name of Nicolas Flamel. He is not, however, a fictional character, but seems to have been a real person (although references to him are scarce), living in France between 1330 and possibly 1418.

While on the road to the holy shrine at Santiago de Compostela in Spain, he met with a convert (a Jewish person who had changed their faith to Christianity) who showed him wonderful things and taught him alchemical skills. One thing that the convert gave Flamel was a 24-page text called *The Book of Abraham the Mage*, which was said to contain instructions for creating the Philosopher's Stone – a magical stone that could turn base metal into gold and grant immortality. It was believed that Flamel found the stone and used it to make himself wealthy. He also wrote a number of books on magic and alchemy, one of which appeared in London in 1624 entitled *Exposition of the Hieroglyphicall Figures,* which reputedly contained instructions for the creation of the Stone.

Although the date of Flamel's death is usually given as 1418, nobody is really sure when he died. Legend says that a grave-robber broke into his tomb in order to steal gold that had been reputedly buried with him, and found it empty.

Since then there have been many sightings claimed. He was alleged to have been seen at a theater in Paris around 1776 and in London during World War I. Some believe he is still living today. Perhaps the Philosopher's Stone has made him immortal. Who knows?

FAR LEFT *A portrait of Nicholas Flamel in old age.* LEFT *Nicholas Flamel in his laboratory working with alchemical secrets.*

JOHN DIMOND

It seems that few wizards in America are well known outside their hometowns. The celebrated "Magician of Marblehead," John Dimond, however, is perhaps an exception. To some he was a strange eccentric, but there were others, especially those who lived closest to him, who feared him greatly as a powerful wizard.

Marblehead is a quaint and peaceful fishing town on the north Massachusetts coast. It has a fine reputation as the birthplace of the American Navy, but it also has another, darker reputation that is connected with witchcraft.

It was here that John Dimond was born. The date of his birth is unknown, but it is thought to have

BELOW *Tales of demons abounded during the time of the witch trials.*

been around 1692, the year of the Salem witch trials where, from June to September, nineteen men and women were convicted of witchcraft and hanged, including an 80-year old man who was pressed to death under heavy stones for refusing to submit to a trial on charges of witchcraft. Hundreds of others faced accusations of witchcraft, while dozens more were imprisoned for months without trial. It was, therefore, an auspicious time and place for a wizard to be born.

For most of his life John lived in a big colonial house in Little Harbor, Marblehead. Even as a young man he was considered "strange," slipping into eerie trances in which he would neither speak nor eat, but emerged from them with a curious knowledge of events far away.

When John's father died, he inherited a small amount of money, which allowed him to buy some land. To the amazement of local people, the land he chose to purchase was a densely wooded area on the edge of the town's Old Burying Ground. His neighbors immediately began to suspect occult motives. It was less than thirty years since the Salem witch trials and the odor of witchcraft was still in the air. There were rumors that Dimond dug up corpses from the graveyard for use in occult experiments and magical spells, but nothing could be proved.

Dimond's strange powers came out when a neighbor, the Widow Brown, complained to him that her firewood had been stolen. Dimond entered one of his now famous trances and, on recovering, confronted the culprit. The man denied the charge, but Dimond "so charmed him" that he was forced to walk through the streets of Marblehead with a log on his back, thus proclaiming himself a thief. Soon after, other people visited the

BELOW *Marblehead Harbor was a peaceful and uneventful place until people began to talk.*

big colonial house, asking the wizard to find stolen or lost items. Sometimes Dimond helped them and other times he didn't, but when he did, his powers of detection and recovery were remarkable.

The "Magician of Marblehead" seemed to have other powers, too. Sometimes he would go up to the Old Burying Ground (some said to converse with the dead), and from the wooded hill he would call out

to ships out on the sea and would intone things like, "Captain Jasper McClelland of the *Elizabeth Anne*, do you hear me? Steer four degrees to starboard and run true until you reach the Halfway Rock," or,

"Captain Benjamin Rowe of the *Hetty*, hear my words. Move six degrees to port or you will founder on a hidden shoal." And by some supernatural means, the captains of these vessels heard him and followed his instructions. For hours Dimond would sit on the hill roaring his commands, calling each captain by name. Some were known to him and some were not, but he got every captain and vessel correct. It was said that he could also sink ships. He had a famous dispute with Micah Taylor, captain of the *Kestrel*, which one day sailed out of Marblehead Harbor and never returned.

Nobody is exactly sure when John Dimond died, but his legacy still lingers on in the coastal town. A local Marblehead highschool sports team that plays in the Northeastern Conference are named "The Magicians," and when a storm rolls in from the sea, local elders say "the Wizard Dimond is up on his hill again." Who knows, he may well be.

LEFT *Following the widespread executions, the legacy of the Salem witch trials was a mighty distrust and fear of magic and the unknown.*

THE COMTE DE St. GERMAIN

Perhaps no figure in history has been more mysterious than the Comte de St. Germain, who is supposed to have lived between 1710 and 1784, although the date of his death — if indeed he did die — is also a mystery. Even who he might have been remains a mystery.

In the first place, it is not clear if he was indeed a Count. Some say that he was the son of Charles II of Spain (born to his widow after the King's death), while others say that he was the son of Francis Rákóczi II, Prince of Transylvania. Others still claim he was someone else entirely. He is described as a courtier, an adventurer, an amateur composer, a musician, an alchemist – and a wizard.

The Comte traveled through Europe in the 1700s visiting many influential people and even some of the royal families there. However, he remained extremely tight-lipped about his own background, telling each person a slightly different story concerning his origins. He was also known to be attracted to the occult and claimed to be a magician of some standing. With some people, he claimed to have known Merlin; with others he claimed to have worked with the thirteenth-century alchemist Roger Bacon and with Dr. John Dee more than two hundred years before. He further claimed that he had visited wizards living in the high mountains of Transylvania or in the deep forests of Germany and that he had studied with them and learned their secrets. For long periods, he would disappear and then would unexpectedly turn up

Right Acquaintances of the Comte de St. Germain claimed that he never ate and that he did not age.

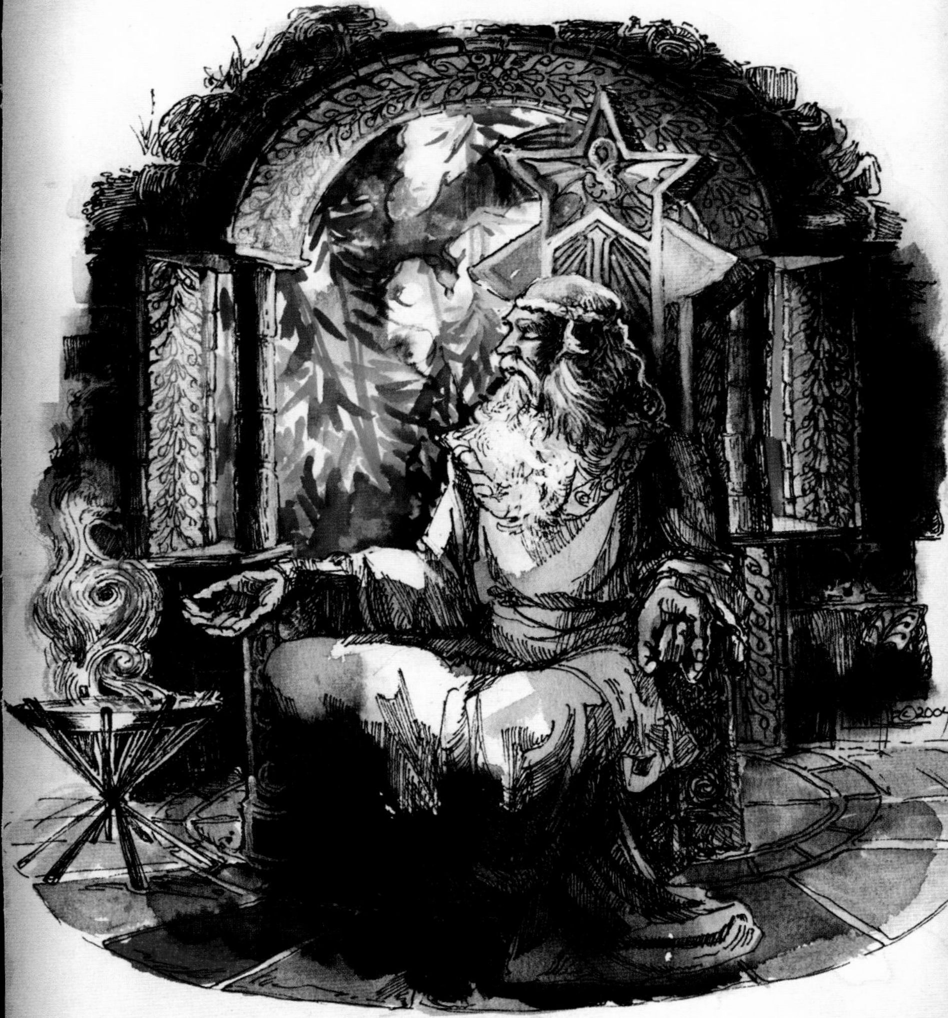
©2004

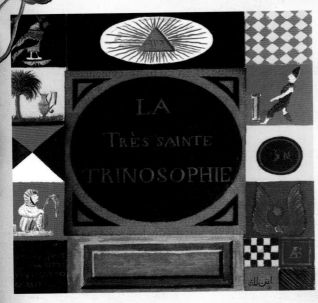

RIGHT *This is the cover of the Comte de St. Germain's book, which was a work on alchemical secrets.*

seemed to know where his money came from – and also eternal youth.

Over time his stories became more and more wild. He boasted that he had lived before, and that in previous incarnations he had been the ruler of an ancient prehistoric kingdom in the Sahara, the Biblical prophet Samuel, the Greek philosopher Plato, and Christopher Columbus, among others.

again. Many of those who met him claimed, although he had been away for years, that he never seemed to age.

This led the Comte to make one of his most staggering claims. In the course of his alchemical studies, he said he had actually found the Philosopher's Stone that other alchemists, such as Nicolas Flamel (see pages 64–65), had been searching for. This, he stated, had given him great wealth – nobody

Astonishingly, he also sometimes boasted that he was immortal, which gave him a certain status among some of the people he visited, particularly if they were interested in the occult and had their own desires to live forever.

He became known in circles of would-be magicians as a wonder-worker and is supposed to have published a number of books on magic. One of these was called *The Most Holy Trinosophia of the Count de St. Germaine* (trinosophia means "threefold wisdom"). Later, those who were interested in the occult and in him would always refer to him as "Master R" (meaning Master Rákóczi, his Transylvanian name) and claimed that his name, St. Germain, came from the Latin *Sanctus Germanus*, meaning "Holy Brother."

Despite his great boasts, he is supposed to have died around 1784, although nobody witnessed his demise and no one is sure if he actually died.

The Comte enjoyed perhaps his greatest fame around the late 1800s/early 1900s. A society dedicated to the occult called the Theosophists, led by a rather colorful woman called H.P. Blavatsky, named him as one of the "Great Masters of Ancient Wisdom" and a guardian of mysterious knowledge. They believed that he was an agent of secret masters high in the Himalayas who had been sent to guide the world toward greater truths. Maybe he was, but even today the Comte de St. Germain remains a figure swathed in mystery.

ABOVE *Helena Petrovna Blavatsky traveled the world, impressing people with her psychic abilities as a medium.*

ADAM WEISHAUPT

One of the most important wizards of the eighteenth century was a German named Adam Weishaupt. He is considered important because he mixed sorcery and politics and is said to have founded a secret magical society that was allegedly dedicated to the overthrow of monarchies and ruling the world through a mixture of sorcery and science.

Weishaupt was born in Ingolstadt, Bavaria, Germany in 1748. His father, Georg, died when Adam was five and he came under the protection of his godfather, Johann Freiherr von Ickstatt, who was a professor of law. Weishaupt entered a local Jesuit school when he was seven and, with a taste for law and politics, he enrolled in the University of Ingolstadt to study the subject in 1768.

He was a brilliant student and emerged at age 20 with a full professorship, later becoming a professor of canon (religious) law with the backing of the Jesuits – Catholic priests famed for their passion for education. However, he also had a darker side to his interests, and in 1776 he formed and led a group known as the Order of Perfectibilists, by whom he was known as Brother Spartacus.

This group – all of whom were brilliant men – were supposed to share secret knowledge, and their main aim was the overthrowing of the great monarchies of Europe by whatever means they could,

including the use of magic. It was said that Weishaupt used very ancient scrolls to invoke certain spells against some of the leading politicians of the day. He also had connections with the Masonic Lodge and was inducted into one of the lodges in Munich in 1777.

However, he was now speaking about certain Gnostic teachings quite openly to his students. The Gnostics were a controversial group of early Christian mystics who were later regarded as heretics – unbelievers – by the Church. Weishaupt spoke

ADAM WEISHAVPT.

RIGHT *Adam Weishaupt, the philosopher, founded one of the most influential societies, the Illuminati.*

about "perfecting humans" through a combination of mysticism and magic, and once again repeated his plan to create a better world. This was of course regarded as treason by the German authorities, and in 1784 Weishaupt was sacked from his job lecturing at the University. To save himself from arrest, he was forced to flee to a remote part of Germany.

He hid in the town of Gotha, where he was given protection by Duke Ernest II of Saxe-Gotha-Altenburg, who looked upon Weishaupt as a great sage and magician. While in Gotha, Weishaupt reformed his magical-political group, which he now called the Illuminati (or the Enlightened). Their purpose was, as before, to take over large areas of the world and to create a perfect human society through magic and mystical teaching. Many of their principles were as they had been when they were originally founded in Bavaria in 1776.

Weishaupt continued to write and publish a number of books that circulated in Europe during the late 1700s and early 1800s. He was able to do so under the kindly influence of Duke Ernest II, who may also have been one of the Illuminati.

The Illuminati's secret knowledge expanded and they kept contact with the Masons and may well have influenced some forms of Scottish Masonry, which were a little different from the mainstream movement. For a while the society that Weishaupt had created was legal and drew some of the most learned men of the day. Later, the authorities became fearful of some of its teachings (and its magic) and banned it, driving it underground.

LEFT *The Masons met in specially built temples like this one in Italy.*

RIGHT *This Roman mosaic shows symbols of the afterlife that were important to the Masons.*

Weishaupt died in 1830 but left a great legacy behind him. The secret society of magicians and scientists – and powerful men – had spread out into the wider world and is rumored to still exist today. Perhaps they might be conspiring to take over the world through magic even now.

GLOSSARY

Alchemy
The science of the Middle Ages that was a combination of magic and chemistry.

Assassins
A secret society of Muslims in the Middle East, from about 1090 to 1272, led by Hasan ibu-al-Sabbah.

Astronomy
The scientific study of the universe beyond the Earth's atmosphere.

Bedouin
One of the nomadic tribes of Arabs that wander the deserts of Africa and Asia.

Black magic or dark arts
Sorcery that is used for evil purposes.

Demonology
The study of, or belief in, demons or fiends.

Djinn
A spirit capable of appearing in human and animal form.

Druid
A member of an ancient order of pre-Christian priests among the Celts of Britain, Ireland, and Gaul.

Dybukk
In Jewish folklore, the soul of a dead person that attaches itself and possesses the body of a living person.

Elixir
A liquid containing a medicinal drug; an alchemical remedy.

Gnostics
An early Christian group that claimed to have special knowledge about spiritual matters.

Golem
In Jewish folklore, a figure made from clay in the form of a human being and brought to life by supernatural means.

Heresy
Any opinion or belief that is considered contrary to the beliefs of the Church.

Illuminati
Originally a religious group in sixteenth-century Spain, this was a name adopted by a secret society founded in Bavaria in 1776.

Mystic
Someone with occult power.

Necromancy
Magic that is practiced by a sorcerer or witch in order to conjure up the dead to obtain knowledge from them.

Occult
To do with magic or the supernatural arts.

Philosopher's Stone
The imagined substance capable of turning other metals into gold.

Ritual
A ceremony, particularly of a religious nature.

Scrying
Divining future events using reflective substances such as crystals, stones, glass, mirrors, water, fire, or smoke.

Shaman
A sorcerer or medicine man who acts as an intermediary between the natural and supernatural worlds.

Trance
A hypnotic state resembling sleep.

Witchcraft
The art or practices of a sorcerer or witch.

ÌПDEX

Index continued

Acknowledgments

Marshall Editions would like to thank the following for their kind permission to reproduce their images:

t = top   **b** = bottom   **c** = center   **r** = right   **l** = left

Cover Credits: Front cover design by Tim Scrivens – Jacket photos: Shutterstock/Getty Images

Pages: 1 Shutterstock/James Steidl; 3 Bridgeman Art Library/Musee de Tesse, Le Mans/Giraudon; **4-5 montage:** Shutterstock/Anyka/Aleks.k/Bruno Passigatti; **6-7** Shutterstock/Samazur; 8 Bridgeman Art Library/Index/La Coveta Alta de la Roca del Lladoner en Valltorta; 9 Art Archive/Bibliothèque des Arts Décoratifs Paris/Gianni Dagli Orti; 10 Shutterstock/Slava Gerj; 11 Shutterstock/Oez; 12 Shutterstock/Dave Nevodka; 13 Bridgeman Art Library/Private Collection/The Stapleton Collection; 14 Bridgeman Art Library/ Private Collection/The Stapleton Collection; 15 Topfoto/Charles Walker; 17 Art Archive/University Library, Istanbul/Gianni Dagli Orti; 18 Art Archive/Biblioteca Estense Modena/Gianni Dagli Orti; **19t** Shutterstock/Christos Georghiou; **19b** Bridgeman Art Library/Private Collection/The Stapleton Collection; 21 Bridgeman Art Library/The British Library; 22 Bridgeman Art Library/The British Library; 23 Bridgeman Art Library/Private Collection/ Christie's Images; **24l** Shutterstock/Dmitrijs Bindemanis; **24br** Corbis/Sygma/Franco Origlia; 25 Corbis/Stefano Bianchetti; 26 akg-images; 27 Scala, Florence; **28-29** Shutterstock/Samazur; 31 Bridgeman Art Library/Private Collection/The Stapleton Collection; **32-33** Corbis/Hulton-Deutsch Collection; **34** akg-images/The British Library; 35 Bridgeman Art Library/The British Library; 36 Bridgeman Art Library/Private Collection; 39 Art Archive/Palazzo Pitti, Florence/Gianni Dagli Orti; 40 Bridgeman Art Library/Institute of Oriental Studies, St. Petersburg; 41 Bridgeman Art Library/Private Collection/The Stapleton Collection; 42 Bridgeman Art Library/Église Saint-Laurent, Salon-de-Provence/Giraudon; 43 Art Archive/Musée Rolin Autun/Alfredo Dagli Orti; 44 Bridgeman Art Library/Musée Nationale des Arts et Traditions Populaires, Paris/Archives Charmet; 45 Art Archive/Biblioteca Augusta Perugia/Gianni Dagli Orti; 46 Art Archive/Bibliothèque des Arts Décoratifs, Paris/Gianni Dagli Orti; 47 Bridgeman Art Library/Bibliotheque des Arts Décoratifs, Paris/Archives Charmet; 48 Bridgeman Art Library/Leeds Museums & Galleries/City Art Gallery; 49 akg-images; 50 Bridgeman Art Library/Ashmolean Museum, University of Oxford; 51 Bridgeman Art Library/Neue Galerie, Kassel Museumslandschaft Hessen Kasse; 52 Bridgeman Art Library/Private Collection; 53 Bridgeman Art Library/ Bibliothèque Nationale, Paris/Archives Charmet; 54 Bridgeman Art Library/Detroit Institute of Arts/Founders Society purchase with Mr & Mrs Bert L. Smokler & Mr & Mrs Lawrence A. Fleischman funds; 55 Scala, Florence/White Images; **56-57** Bridgeman Art Library/Musee des Beaux-Arts, Nantes/Giraudon; 58 Scala, Florence/Kunsthistorisches Museum/Austrian Archives; 59 Shutterstock/Fribus Ekaterina; 61 Alamy/North Wind Picture Archives; 63 Art Archive/Biblioteca Nazionale Marciana Venice/Gianni Dagli Orti; 64 Bridgeman Art Library/ Musee de la Ville de Paris, Musée Carnavalet/Giraudon; 65 Art Archive/Ca Rezzonico Museum, Venice/Gianni Dagli Orti; 66 Bridgeman Art Library/Private Collection/© Look & Learn; 67 Topfoto/The Granger Collection; **68-69** Bridgeman Art Library/Private Collection/The Stapleton Collection; 71 Shutterstock/Lynette; 72 Bridgeman Art Library/Bibliothèque Municipale, Troyes/Archives Charmet; 73 Topfoto/The Granger Collection; 74 Topfoto/Alinari; 75 Mary Evans Picture Library; 76 Art Archive/Museo Civico Turin; 77 Art Archive/Bibliothèque des Arts Décoratifs Paris/Gianni Dagli Orti.